Faerie Lights

JILLIAN SAWYER

Photography
Chris Garnett

Published by
The Original Redback Press

Printed in Western Australia

This book was always for you Sigi!
Friendship never needs words, it lives in our hearts, our feelings and our deeds.
Thank you for being my friend.

Published by The Original Redback Press
Telephone 61 9 481 4991
Facsimile 61 9 481 4991
July 1995.
Reprinted November 1995.

FOREWORD

Each of us finds at some stage in our life, there comes a time when we need some form of release. Those of us who enjoy working with stained glass, know that it helps to fulfil the spiritual side of our nature and returns us refreshed to our usual routine. Weaving stories around my childhood visions of Faeries, they took on a mature new life of their own, and in their creation I found a great deal of satisfaction and a curious sense of peace.

So from the creatures of the icebound mountains, lakes and fjords of Scandinavia and the dark woods of Europe, to the wild folk of Celtic fable and ancient Britain, from the strange beings of Ireland and the magic of Merlin of Arthurian legend, to the sweet little faerie at the bottom of the garden, come my Faeries.

Faerie legends from ages past abound and have always been part of folklore. What was fact and what was fantasy, has been distorted and interwoven by the mists of time. We were closer to the earth then, more at one with nature, and who knows what creatures walked with us and talked with us? Now we have lost those links with nature and we no longer see or hear.

Whose loss? Theirs or ours? Ours I think!

I know a land where Faeries still exist - in the valleys of my mind,

alive and vibrant and where I can see them at will.

Maybe you see them too?

Jillian Sawyer

Firebird Leadlights

P.O. Box 522 Cannington WA 6107

Fax & Tel (09) 362 6259

June 1995

ATHENA
QUEEN OF PARADISE JUNGLE

Come quickly to Paradise Jungle
to hide 'neath its sheltering leaves.
Come, Flee to my Paradise home,
safe under the spell that it weaves.
For the witching hour is upon us
and now is the time to be near.
For out of the shadows of the old spooky hollow
come the trolls and ogres we fear.

XANIANE
THE CRYSTAL WARRIOR

With crystal shard she guards the Portal
Sad in her charge, but fierce in her beauty,
for she knows if whoever enters, be he Mortal,
Then Faerie is lost and she has failed in her duty.
Her duty.

ATHENA
QUEEN OF PARADISE JUNGLE

TECHNICAL DETAILS

Careful consideration of grain of glass to follow natural
movement of hair, dress, foliage, etc. will enhance
finished article. Hanging loop is tinned copper wire.
Correct placement of hanging loop is between the flower
petals. Features have been painted with black enamel.
Edge Beading (built up edge of solder) for strength and
durability.

GLASS CHOICE:
Wings - Clear hammered and iridised blue
Skintone - Light amber machined antique
Hair - Black baroque
Dress - Orange streaky with orange frill
Foliage - Shades of green
Flower - Orange, blue, blue-green

XANIANE
THE CRYSTAL WARRIOR

TECHNICAL DETAILS

Hanging loop between hair and main wing. Shoulder clasp is a small faceted jewel. Belt Jewel is a rainbow cabochon. Glass cut runs under waist rope and twisted copperwire ropes are attached over this seam, then the lower ropes are just overlaid and attached to side seams. Spear - A Crystal in a jewellery finding and soldered to a 3mm brass rod. This is soldered between hair and cape on right side and more rod soldered over wing into seams on left side for 3D effect. Features painted with white enamel. Edge beading.

GLASS CHOICE:
Wings - Multicoloured streaky granite
Hair - White baroque
Dress - Shades of amber
Skintone - Brown mouthblown antique

WHISPER
PRINCESS OF INNOCENCE

*Princess of innocence, childish wonder
and enchantment, she is forever untouched
by the evils of the outside world.*

AEOLEAN
THE WIND DANCER

Airy and insubstantial as the bubbles she chases.
Is that her reflection on the surface tension?
As the bubble bursts, she is gone.
Did I really see her?

9

WHISPER
PRINCESS OF INNOCENCE

TECHNICAL DETAIL

Flower in hair is an old jewellery finding
soldered into place when piece is completed.
Hanging loop positioned between wings. Edge
Beading. Features painted on face and hands
with black enamel.

GLASS CHOICE:
Hair - Pink baroque
Dress - Aqua and pale amber
Skintone - Flesh
Wings - Gold/aqua

AEOLEAN
THE WIND DANCER

1

2 3

4

TECHNICAL DETAILS

Bubbles 1,2,3 and 4 are completed with edge beading and attached
with solder over remaining bubbles for a three dimensional effect.
Face of Aeolean left free of foil for added effect (just carefully ground
using 5ml grinding head). Wing filaments begun within main body of
wings for maximum design strength. Features painted with black
enamel. Edge beading.

GLASS CHOICE:

Skintone - Green
Hair - Green streaky
Dress - Flashed white
Wing Filaments - Gold/pink mouthblown antique
Wing Segments - Gold/pink mouthblown antique
Main Wings - Iridised pink streaky
Bubbles - Iridised clear baroque

11

MOONGLOW

Perched there so prettily on your fine pearly shell,
see how it mirrors the moon so well
Your delicate wild beauty is a joy to behold
and you've sprinkled the stardust so your hair glints with gold
You've captured the moonbeams like gossamer threads
and dangled them there so their shine gently spreads.

MISTY
THE NYMPH OF THE LILYPADS

I caught her there just as she stepped from her morning bath.
Covering quickly with her wispy towel,
she flashed me a bashful grin and was gone!

MOONGLOW

TECHNICAL DETAILS

Wing spines are tinned copperwire soldered into seams and along leading edge of wings. Hanging loop positioned behind spine on top wing. Features painted with black enamel. Edge beading for strength and durability.

GLASS CHOICE:
Hair - Blue/gold
Body - Flesh
Inner Wings - Clear crackle glass
Outer Wings - Clear alt deutsch
Spines - Iridised clear granite
Dress - Pink opaque
Shell - Pearlised white
Leaves - Moss green

MISTY
NYMPH OF THE LILYPADS

TECHNICAL DETAILS

Hanging loops tinned copperwire positioned at hair and wing joint. Solder blob for enhancement of breast. Edge beading. Features painted with black enamel.

GLASS CHOICE:
Hair - Chestnut (dark amber)
Skintone - Flesh
Wings - Gold/pink mouthblown antique, iridised clear baroque
Towel - Milky pink
Lily - Cream opaque
Lilypad and Stem - Shades of green

BUTTERCUP

Oh sweet little Butterfly lady
what are you thinking as you sit on your chair?
So full of grace is your kind loving face
but one sees the sadness lingering there.
The sadness is for the child who is lost
Who else but you will care?
You will comfort and cuddle and right from the start,
the soul who is lost you will take to your heart.

16

TALIEN

Spell Maker
Dream Taker
Carry me, Carry me home
I long to be there for lost was I here
and never more will I roam.

BUTTERCUP

TECHNICAL DETAILS

Hanging loop positioned between hair and wings. Hair ribbon
- glass cut in one piece with overlaid twists of tinned
copperwire soldered into seams. Edge beading. Face carefully
ground with small grinding head and left bare edged for
effect. Features painted with fine brush and black enamel as
final touch.

GLASS CHOICE:
Skintone - Flesh
Wings - Tan, deep brown and orange
Hair - Amber streaky
Gown - Yellow opaque
Rocks - Grey opaque
Mushroom stems - Wine
Mushroom Caps - Dusky rose
Mushroom Flesh - Pink baroque

TALIEN

TECHNICAL DETAILS

Placement of glass for wing feathers crucial for maximum effect, therefore some glass wastage. Tinned copperwire attached to iridised glass and plain tinned copperwire used as wing filaments. These are in turn soldered to wings and positioned at differing heights to give 3D effect. Hanging loop positioned behind wing filament at wing and hair joint. Edge beading.

GLASS CHOICE:
Wings - Blue green streaky
Wing Feathers - Blue glue chip
Wing Filaments - Iridised blue
Dress - Aqua/white, aqua/amber opaque
Skintone - Flesh
Hair - Black baroque

WILLOW

*From her watery home she rises, to frolic
and play as any nymph would
Twisting and twining flowers and leaves of all sizes,
whipping around as quick as she could
and gathering momentum, off the buds fly
to land on the water and gently float by.
Slowly spinning and turning at the currents soft mercy
They reach the far shore to become cups for the
thirsty.*

STARBRIGHT

As the first fires of sunrise appear in the sky
I wait and I watch
and by the light of the red morning star
I am privileged to witness a miracle of wonder,
The birth of the First Butterfly.

TECHNICAL DETAILS

Flower stems heavy gauge tinned copperwire soldered and attached to appear to twine around body. Cut into sections and joined at flower bases and hair to eventually meet the wing. Stamens are tinned, solderfilled copperwire loops. Hanging loop positioned between hair strands. Edge Beading. After piece is completed paint features on hands and face.

GLASS CHOICE:
Flowers - Pink/clear streaky
Foliage - Shades of green
Skintone - Light blue machined antique
Hair - Amber reamy
Wings - Clear waterglass

STARBRIGHT

TECHNICAL DETAILS

Butterfly has bent tinned copperwire for legs and antennae (which have applied solder blobs).
Butterfly constructed separately and soldered behind hands as if landing. Detail on hands
obtained through use of overlaid copperfoil. Face left free of foil for effect. Wing spines are
tinned wire attached along edge and hidden under edge beading. Features painted.

GLASS CHOICE:
Wings - Clear obscure and pink/clear streaky
Hair - Pink/clear streaky
Dress - Multicoloured pink streaky opaque
Flower - Yellow/white opaque and
           yellow opaque
Skintone - Light amber machined antique
Foliage - Green/amber streaky
Butterfly Wings - Iridised blue
Butterfly Body - Black baroque

23

BREEZE

*Flower softly sways and leaf gently bends as
you settle yourself and curl your dainty wings
out of harms way.
For when the storyteller comes and weaves her
spell, it's time to laze awhile and lose the day
in dreams of other times.*

BLUEWING

*Oh Faerie Bluewing please
Tread softly,
Stand quietly,
Listen, hear the whisperings?
Peer silently from behind the leaves
and you might see the shy sprites of
the first sunbeams, before they flee.*

TECHNICAL DETAILS

Placement of glass for wings is critical for maximum effect. Side curls in hair constructed from twisted soldered copperwire. Curl twining over breast conceals a glass cut. Hanging loop positioned where petal and leaf meet. Features painted with black enamel. Edge beading essential.

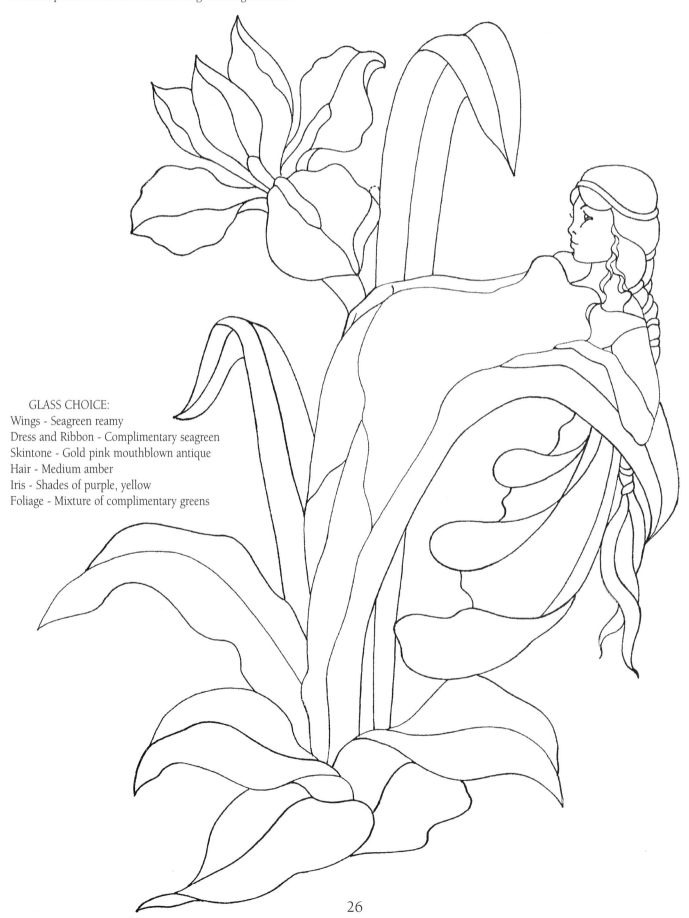

GLASS CHOICE:
Wings - Seagreen reamy
Dress and Ribbon - Complimentary seagreen
Skintone - Gold pink mouthblown antique
Hair - Medium amber
Iris - Shades of purple, yellow
Foliage - Mixture of complimentary greens

BLUEWING

TECHNICAL DETAILS

Wing streamers begun in main body of wing for maximum strength and also reinforced with copperwire. Stamens are tinned copperwire with solder blobs. Hanging loop positioned at hair and wing joint. Edge beading. Features painted with black enamel.

GLASS CHOICE:
Flower - Peach/white opaque
Hair - Black reamy
Skintone - Flesh machined antique
Wings - Clear obscure and aqua/clear streaky
Dress - Complimentary blue
Foliage - Shades of green

PEACE
LADY OF THE MORNING DEW

Beauty of the morning, she is the keeper of the opening buds, carefully unfolding petals and lifting flowerheads out of the morning mist to meet the first rays of sunshine and greet the sparkling day.

MOONROSE

Quietly on iridescent wings, she invokes her magic rites, to harvest the perfume of the delicate moon rose, before it folds its snow green petals against the day, to await the gentle golden glow of the next springtime moon.

PEACE
LADY OF THE MORNING DEW

TECHNICAL DETAILS

Rose stem is fine sheet copper cut to shape, tinned and built up with solder then joined with solder to glass pieces. Wings are main feature and special attention should be paid to glass choice. Hanging loop positioned at hair and wing joint. Edge beading. Black enamel painted features.

GLASS CHOICE:
Hair - Black reamy
Hair Ornament - Red
Rose - Shades of red
Foliage - Shades of green
Skintone - Flesh machined antique
Dress - Pink opaque
Wings - Iridised clear ripple complimented with clear
    alt deutsch

MOONROSE

TECHNICAL DETAILS

Wing filaments are sheet copper cut to shape with wire attachments partly concealed under built up solder. These tendrils are applied after main soldering is completed. (Tendril hitting sleeve conceals glass cut taken through wing.) Laurel wreath in hair made from old broken brooch. Hanging loop positioned between wings. Edge beading. Black enamel for painted features.

GLASS CHOICE:
Wings - Clear iridised ripple
Hair - Amber streaky
Skintone - Flesh
Dress - Shades of mauve
Flower - White, pale green and lemon opaque
Foliage - Moss green
Stems - Darker green

DYANDRA
FOREST TEMPTRESS

Wild one, Fey one,
Enchant me, elude me,
Entice me away, away to
your forest of green
Leading me, teasing me,
pleasing me
to follow you, follow you on,
Never again to be seen.

FIERYTHORN

*Queen of all things sensuous and exotic.
Incandescent and vibrant, she is intoxicated
by the heady perfumes of the night.*

DYANDRA
FOREST TEMPTRESS

TECHNICAL DETAILS

Heavy gauge tinned copperwire for twining
stems (leading edge of which goes over arm to
conceal glass cut) Hanging loop positioned at
hair and wing joint. Edge beading. Black enamel
for features.

GLASS CHOICE:

Skintone - Flesh

Hair - Dark amber for chestnut toning

Leaves on Dress - Green brown streaky

Dress - Green with complimentary green
        for upturned petals

Foliage - Varying shades of green

Wings - Clear obscure with green/clear streaky

TECHNICAL DETAILS

Flower stems heavy gauge copperwire. Stamens; copperwire with solder blobs. Wing spines are cut from sheet copper and built up with solder then attached during soldering process. Hanging loop positioned between flower and first wing spine. Edge beading. Black enamel for features. Necklace optional.

GLASS CHOICE:
Skintone - Pale green
Hair - Blue/black streaky, black baroque
Wings - Red/yellow streaky
Dress - Shades of orange and yellow
Foliage - Shades of green
Flowers - Shades of blue

Faeries of the Field

FAERIES OF THE FIELD

Come down to the Faerie meadow,
See us swoop and dive in the sun.
We laugh and we sing in our sweet faerie ring,
As we plan the chores to be done.
Then we buzz here and there like the
great bumblebee,
Putting things right in our world
with love and mischievous glee!
We dart like the friendly swallow
and join voice with the lark in the sky
We do all these things for the joy that they bring
and the love of just wanting to try
And the more that we do and the more that we sing,
The greater the joy that we yield.
So this is the life, the love and the fun,
The Faeries of the Field joyful day done!

TECHNICAL DETAIL

Wing filaments tinned copperwire with applied solder blobs then attached at appropriate points. Careful use of grain of glass enhances flow of the hair. Hanging loop positioned between feet. This faerie can also be turned upside down as if she's doing a backflip, in which case the hanging loop is positioned at hair and wing joint. Standard edge beading.

GLASS CHOICE:
Wings - Clear iridised granite
Hair - Black baroque
Skintone - Milky pink

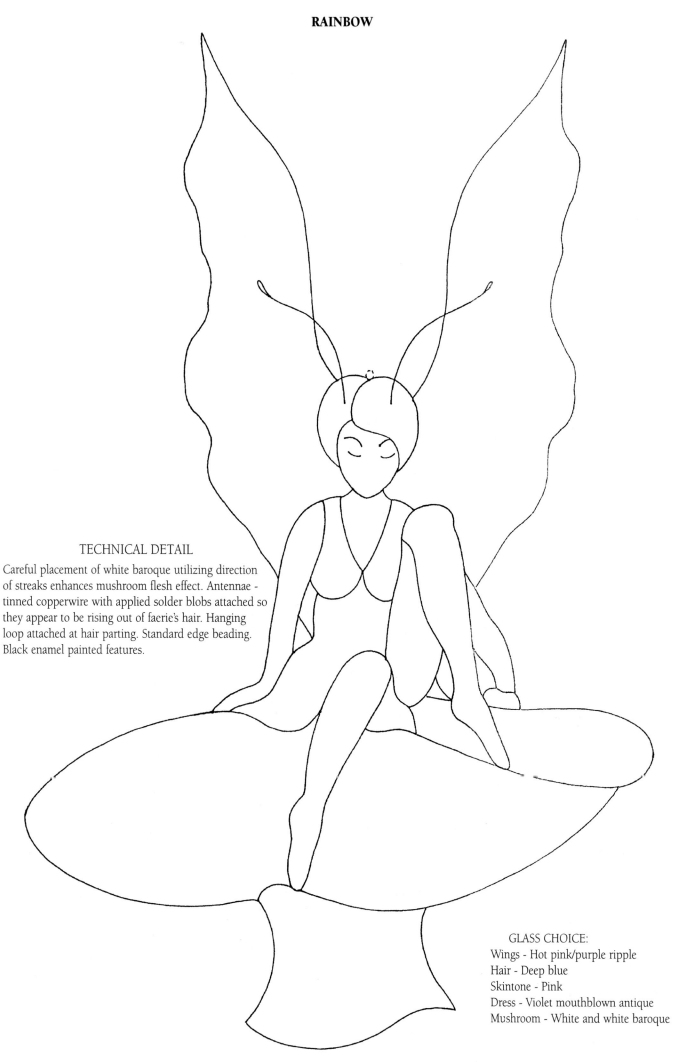

TECHNICAL DETAIL

Careful placement of white baroque utilizing direction of streaks enhances mushroom flesh effect. Antennae - tinned copperwire with applied solder blobs attached so they appear to be rising out of faerie's hair. Hanging loop attached at hair parting. Standard edge beading. Black enamel painted features.

GLASS CHOICE:
Wings - Hot pink/purple ripple
Hair - Deep blue
Skintone - Pink
Dress - Violet mouthblown antique
Mushroom - White and white baroque

FIREFLY

Come down to the Faerie meadow
See us swoop and dive in the sun.

RAINBOW

We laugh and we sing in our sweet Faerie ring
as we plan the chores to be done.

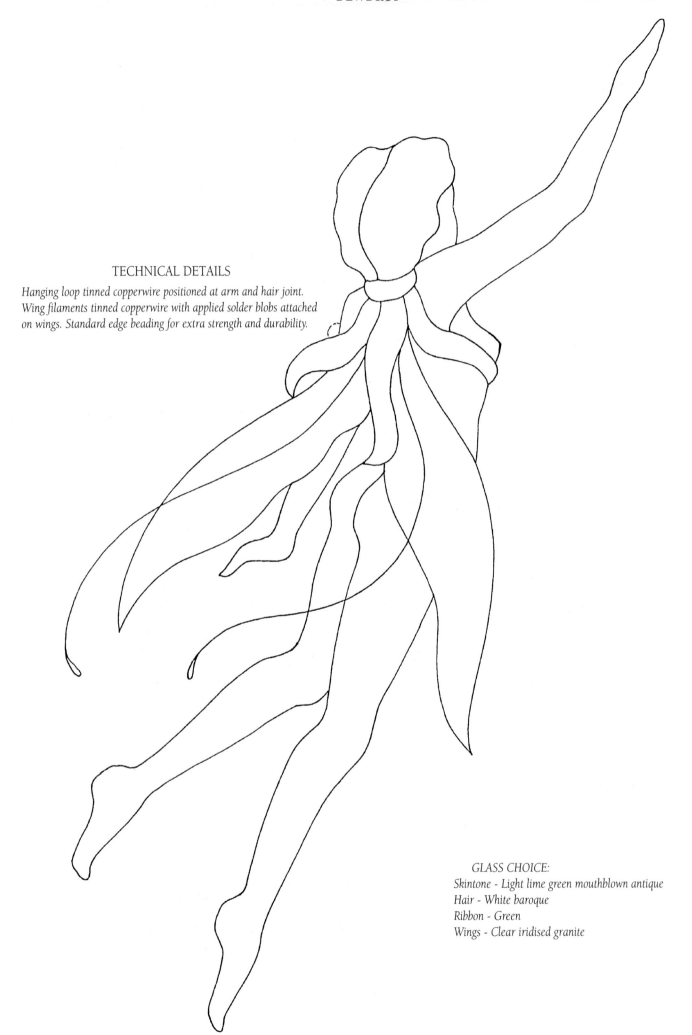

TECHNICAL DETAILS

*Hanging loop tinned copperwire positioned at arm and hair joint.
Wing filaments tinned copperwire with applied solder blobs attached
on wings. Standard edge beading for extra strength and durability.*

GLASS CHOICE:
Skintone - Light lime green mouthblown antique
Hair - White baroque
Ribbon - Green
Wings - Clear iridised granite

TWINKLETOES

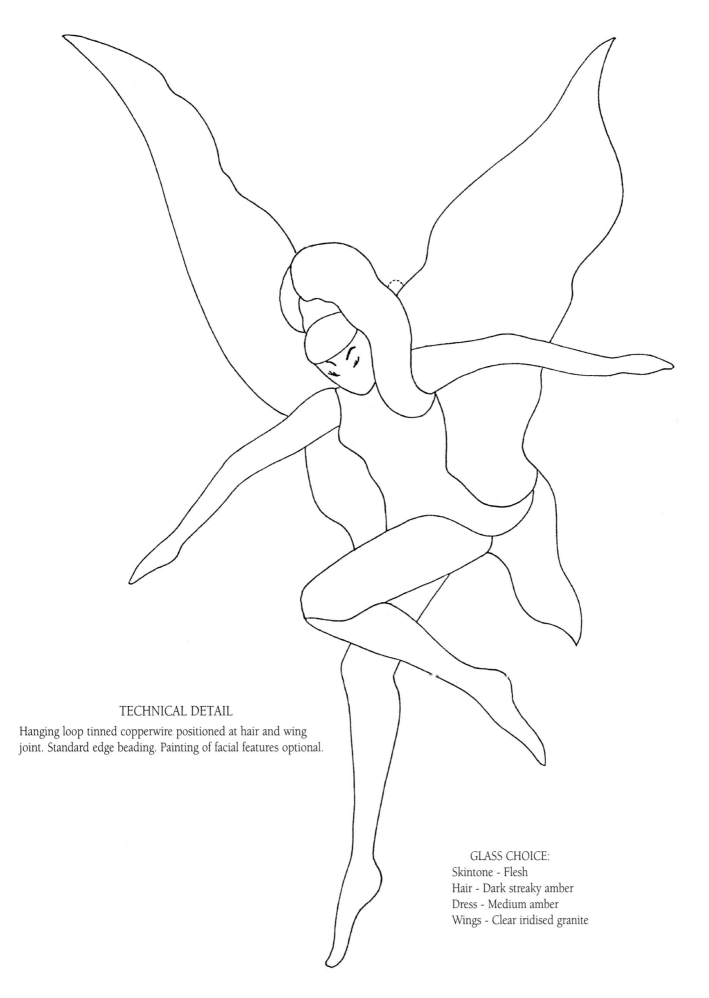

TECHNICAL DETAIL

Hanging loop tinned copperwire positioned at hair and wing
joint. Standard edge beading. Painting of facial features optional.

GLASS CHOICE:
Skintone - Flesh
Hair - Dark streaky amber
Dress - Medium amber
Wings - Clear iridised granite

DEWDROP

Then we buzz here and there like the great bumblebee.

TWINKLETOES

Putting things right in our world
with love and mischievous glee.

SNOWFLAKE

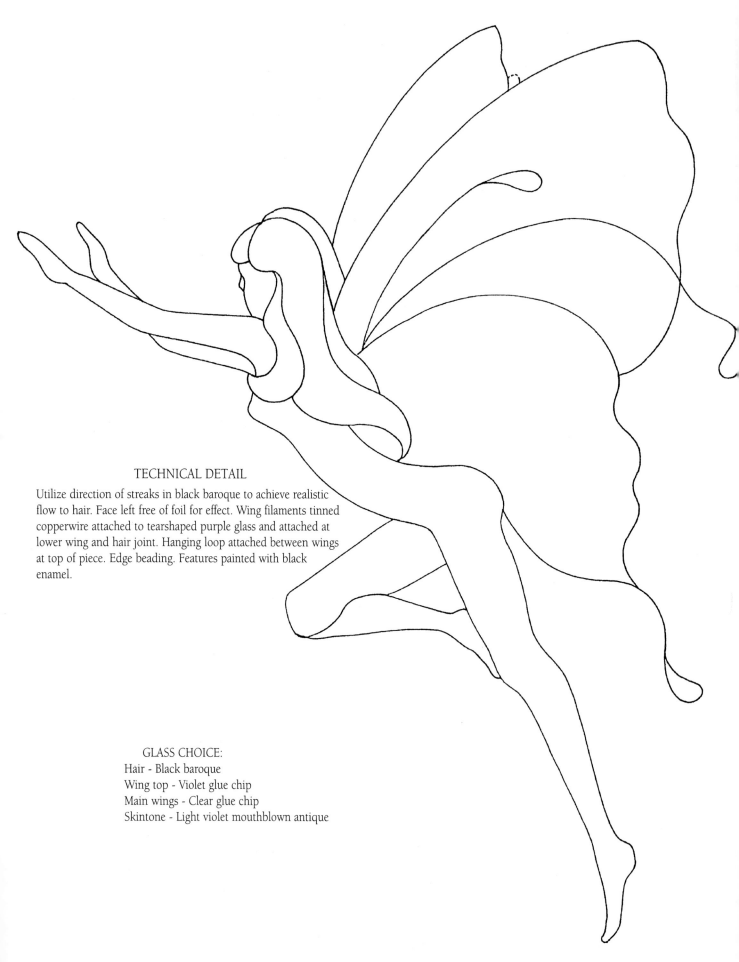

TECHNICAL DETAIL

Utilize direction of streaks in black baroque to achieve realistic
flow to hair. Face left free of foil for effect. Wing filaments tinned
copperwire attached to tearshaped purple glass and attached at
lower wing and hair joint. Hanging loop attached between wings
at top of piece. Edge beading. Features painted with black
enamel.

GLASS CHOICE:
Hair - Black baroque
Wing top - Violet glue chip
Main wings - Clear glue chip
Skintone - Light violet mouthblown antique

SUNDEW

TECHNICAL DETAIL

Best advantage taken of black baroque for use in hair. Hair ornament
is broken earing attached with solder when piece completed.
Hanging loop positioned behind hair ornament. Wing filaments
attached along edge of wing and concealed under edge beading.
Edge beading.

GLASS CHOICE:
Hair - Black baroque
Skintone - Gold pink mouthblown antique
Wings - Clear iridised ripple
Mushroom - Pink/green/white opaque, white baroque and
flashed white

SNOWFLAKE

We dart like the friendly swallow
and join voice with the lark in the sky.

SUNDEW

We do all these things for the joy that they bring
and the love of just wanting to try.

TECHNICAL DETAIL

Wing filaments tinned copperwire with solder blobs attached at hair and also
at edge of wings. Antennae attached at edge of hair to appear to be coming out
of hair. Hanging loop positioned behind wing filament on top wing to obtain
correct angle of landing. Painting of features optional. Edge beading essential,
particularly well built up around left hand and dress joints.

GLASS CHOICE:
Wings - Blue glue chip
Hair - White baroque
Dress - Darker blue than wings
Skintone - Gold pink mouthblown antique

TECHNICAL DETAIL

Utilise flow of baroque glass for effect in wings.
Hanging loop positioned between wings at hair
joint. Copperwire concealed under edge beading
to emphasise flare of dress. Features painted
with black enamel. Edge beading.

GLASS CHOICE:
Hair - Amber streaky
Wings - Sea green baroque
Dress - Iridised seagreen
Skintone - Gold pink antique

SKYE

And the more that we do and the more that we sing,
the greater the joy that we yield

PERIWINKLE

So this is the life, the love and the fun,
The Faeries of the Field joyful day done!

ETCETERA

All Faeries are blown up to A3 size for ease of construction. Faeries of the Field can be smaller than A3.

Let YOUR imagination inspire YOUR glass choice.

Make good use of colour, grain of glass, flow of glass and mixture of glass types and textures. In effect, learn how to paint with your glass. EXPERIMENT! Sometimes, glass used in unexpected ways can add that extra sparkle or lift to your piece. For instance, a monochrome theme can be made startling with the effective use of one brightly opposing colour!

Always use good quality solder and liquid flux (3mm 60/40 solid core wire solder is the best). I use an 80watt soldering iron with an iron clad chisel tip. These tips never need filing and can be retinned if necessary, using a block of solid sal ammoniac. Keep your tip clean during the soldering process by frequently running it through a sponge dampened with water. This impedes the build up of impurities on your solder seam, which can hinder the cleaning and patina process.

Edge beading is used to give your piece extra strength and durability and to produce a finished, professional look. This is achieved by holding your piece on the edge. Using the flat of your tip to apply solder, hold still a few seconds until solder has solidified, then tilt your piece and repeat until you have built up a nice edge all around. Keep the spot you are working on level until solder sets - if you are slightly tilted in either direction, the solder will roll, resulting in an uneven bead. To prevent accidents always support your piece to one side of the area you are beading, never underneath, and wear protective gloves.

To apply solder blobs to the end of tinned wire, hold one end with pliers and pick up a small amount of solder on your iron. Place the tip in contact with the fluxed wire and the solder will run down the wire and form a ball on the end. At this point, remove the iron from the wire and with the heat source removed, the solder blob will solidify. If all steps are followed carefully and with slow, steady movements, you will soon have this procedure under control.

Always clean and patina your piece immediately you have finished soldering to avoid oxidization of seams. Oxidization will impede successful patination.